St. Andrews Sund

Christmas Programs for Children

compiled by

Pat Fittro

STANDARD PUBLISHING

Cincinnati, Ohio

Permission is granted to reproduce this material for
ministry purposes only—not for resale.

The Standard Publishing Company, Cincinnati, Ohio
A division of Standex International Corporation
© 1999 by The Standard Publishing Company

ISBN 0-7847-0956-4

CONTENTS

Something Important
Dixie Phillips

I have something really
   "important" to say,
"Praise God for our Christmas
   play!"

Isn't This True?
Helen Kitchell Evans

Sure, I like to get presents,
  But I like to give them too;
Really, more cheer comes from
  giving
  Than getting. *(Pause.)* Isn't this
  true?

Joseph's Dream
Margaret Primrose

I have had lots of dreams
  That did not make much
  sense,
And to claim some special
  meaning
Would only be pretense.
But when Joseph had a dream,
An angel said, "Do not fear.
Take Mary home as your wife.
  The birth of a Son is near."
"Jesus shall be His name,
  He shall save His people from
  sin—
People of every race,
  Children, women and men."

Blessed Christmas Day
Helen Kitchell Evans

Well, folks, our program is
  over
  We have said all we're
  supposed to say. *(Pause.)*
Except *(Pause.)* I'm to have the
  last word:
  "Have a blessed Christmas
  Day!"

1 the Air
ora M. Owen

ladness was in the air.
reat joy was also there.
he angels praised His name,
/hen baby Jesus came.

hristmas Lights
ell Ford Hann

ountless lights are twinkling,
As Christmas Day draws near;
eflecting brilliance and
   glistening,
With vibrant colors . . . to
   shiny clear.
shades of holiday finery,
Luminous lights of glitz and
   show:
ickering in the evening's
   stillness
Rendering to hearts a soft,
   warm glow.
s we celebrate this holy
   season,
With Christmas joyously
   bright;
e observe and remember
   God's Gift to us,
esus, the ultimate, perfect
   light.

Stopped By to Say
Dixie Phillips

I just stopped by to cheerfully say,
   (Smile.)
"I'm so proud to be in our
   Christmas play!"

What Was It Like?
Margaret Primrose

What was it like when Jesus
   slept
In a manger full of hay?
Were there doves to coo a
   lullaby
And a donkey that liked to
   bray?

Did a spider keep on spinning a
   web
While a draft crept under the
   door?
Was the stable full of animal
   smells
And fogged by dust from the
   floor?

Did children like me run to see
The Babe in the shadowy
   stall?
I think they came, then spread
   the fame
Of the One who is Lord of all.

Good News

Margaret Primrose

Like an angel of long ago
  I come with news of great joy;
For God so loved the world
  That He sent us a baby Boy.

I'm so glad He came to save us,
  That I say what the angels
    said then,
"Glory to God in the highest,
  And . . . peace, good will
    toward men."

Luke 2:14 *(King James Version)*

Words Can't Tell

Cora M. Owen

No words can ever ever tell
  The joy that came that night,
When Jesus came down to the
    earth
  To be this dark world's light.

The words we use cannot
    express
  What happened when He
    came;
When God came down in
    human flesh
  To save us. Praise His name!

A Tiny Baby

Enelle Eder

A tiny baby came,
  Born in a manger stall.
He was a gift from God,
  Sent to one and all.

A tiny baby came
  To little Bethlehem town.
The angels sang about Him
  As His glory shone around.

A tiny baby came
  To fulfill His Father's plan.
To be sin's sacrifice,
  The only hope for man.

The Best Gift

Margaret Primrose

I like Christmas trees
  Standing in the snow
And wearing lights
  That twinkle and glow.

I like packages
  Addressed to me
And stacks of presents
  Under a tree.

But I **love** the baby
  Who was born in a stall;
For Jesus our Savior
  Is the best gift of all.

lory to God
llian Robbins

ome things bring sadness,
   some bring pain,
Others fill us with joy.
ut what comes to the hearts of
   men
At the birth of that miracle
   boy?

sus was born in Bethlehem,
God's own chosen place.
he wonder and amazement of
   the shepherds there
Showed in the light of their face.

he wise men surely filled with
   awe,
Those travelers from days of
   old,
ho came from the east with
   adoration,
Brought frankincense, myrrh
   and gold.

hat do we feel as we
   remember again
he night that Jesus came?
precious baby born that night
With a very special name.

Emmanuel" the angel had said,
Meaning God is with us here,
y in our hearts, peace in our
   souls
To know the Lord is near.

And so our voices ring out for
   all
To praise the name of the
   Lord.
Glory to God and His
   marvelous love
We rejoice in the truth of His
   Word.

A Shepherd Boy's Story
Margaret Primrose

"You're only a boy,"
   My father said.
"Now, go to the tent;
   It's time for bed."

"But, Father," I pleaded,
   "I'll soon be a man.
I want to stay up
   Just to see if I can."

Well, he let me stay,
   So I was here
When we saw a bright light
   And angels appeared.

"Fear not," they told us,
   "There's good news for all.
Go look for a Baby
   Who sleeps in a stall."

Then I found my Savior,
   The King of kings,
Who rules the world
   And created all things.

What We Love

Helen Kitchen Evans

Child 1: I love the pretty lights
That shine upon the tree.

Child 2: I love all the boxes
That are wrapped for me.

Child 3: I love the cards that Mother
Sends to friends and family.

Child 4: I love the cards, too,
Written just for me.

All: We love a lot of things
That bring us joy and cheer.
But most of all we love Jesus
Our Jesus so sweet, so dear.

Why We're Here

Helen Kitchell Evans

Child 1: I'm here to say "Hello" to you,

Child 2: I'm here to do the same;

Child 3: It's merry Christmastime,

Child 4: The time when Jesus came.

All: So here's a wish to all who are here:
Happy Christmas and a good New Year!

I Love Christmas

Lillian Robbins

Child 1:   I love Christmas that comes each year
And gives us smiling faces.

Child 2:   My favorite time is Christmas morn,
Finding gifts in different places.

Child 3:   I really like the Christmas dinner
When we gather around the table.

Child 4:   I remember most the baby Jesus
And the manger in a stable.

Child 5:   I wonder about Mary who held her little Son
And how she sang Him a lullaby.

Child 6:   Was the moon shining up above,
Or just that star in the sky?

Child 7:   How many animals were in that stall?
Maybe there were seven.

Child 8:   Anyway, we know for sure,
God sent His Son from Heaven.

All: Merry Christmas everyone!

God's Christmas Plan
Beverly C. Bishop

A Christmas program for primaries or juniors. Even a small group can present an impressive multimedia program. An overhead projector and a screen or white wall will give the illusion of a major production. Slides or videos may also be used (available through Bible bookstores). A choir of children, teens or adults offers a transition for the twelve children's speaking parts.

VIDEO: Angelic Messenger

Child 1
The angel came
To Mary's home,
To give the news
That Christ would come.

Child 2
She took him at
His word that day,
And trusted God
To lead the way.

VIDEO: Bethlehem
CHOIR: "O Little Town of
      Bethlehem"

Child 3
Before His birth
The prophet said
That Bethlehem
Would hold His bed.

VIDEO: Journey to Bethlehem

Child 4
At Caesar's word
They journeyed far
To Bethlehem.
God gave a star.

VIDEO: Baby in the hay
CHOIR: "Away in a Manger"

Child 5
There was no room
Where they could stay
So Christ was laid
Upon the hay.

Child 6
A manger was
His baby bed;
It was the place
Where cows were fed.

VIDEO: Shepherds
CHOIR: "While Shepherds
Watched Their Flocks"
or "Hark! the Herald
Angels Sing"

Child 7
The shepherds saw
The angel throng,
They saw the light
And heard the song.

Child 8
When Christ was born
The shepherds came
Because the angels
Told His fame.

VIDEO: The Wise men come
CHOIR: "We Three Kings"

Child 9
God chose a star
To show the way
To Bethlehem,
Where Jesus lay.

VIDEO: Star
CHOIR: "Silent Night! Holy
Night!"

Child 10
A zillion stars
Shone in the sky
But His was special,
Way up high.

VIDEO: Wise men present
their gifts

Child 11
The wise men came
With gifts and love
To see the Christ child
From above.

VIDEO: Jesus on the cross

Child 12
When Christ was born
It was the plan
That He would die
For sinful man.

CHOIR: "Thou Didst Leave
Thy Throne" or "The
Old Rugged Cross"

More Than This

Carolyn R. Scheidies

Characters:
Ben, elementary age
Sally, Ben's sister, teenage
Jared, Sally's friend, teenage
Mary, Joseph, and Shepherds
Preschoolers
Primaries
Juniors

Setting: Contemporary and Bible times

Props: Christmas tree, presents, sofa, phone, table, Bible, manger, cards to
   spell J-E-S-U-S, costumes for Mary, Joseph, and Shepherds

Scene 1

*Contemporary living room setting, night before Christmas. Ben, Sally, and Jared
around the Christmas tree. Ben sits on the floor, Sally and Jared on a sofa facing
the tree.*

Ben *(picking up presents and shaking them):* Gotta see. Gotta see,
   What's here for me.

(Phone rings. Sally answers it.)

Sally: Mom. Yes, we're fine. Jared's still here and we're all safe. And yes,
   Ben is still up. *(Pauses, listens.)* You'll be late? *(Pause.)* I got you. Will
   do, Mom. *(Pause.)* You and Dad have a good time. Bye. *(Hangs up.)*
   That was Mom, Ben. She said it is time for you to go to bed.
Ben: I don't like what Mama said,
   It's Christmas Eve. I don't wanta go to bed!
Jared: Does he always talk like this, in rhyme, I mean?
Sally: Afraid so, Jared. *(Shrugs.)* Some of it's pretty good. Come on, little
   brother. *(Starts to get up.)*

Ben *(pleading):* Please, Sally, please let me sleep by the lights and the tree,
 I want to watch Christmas come. Don't you see?
Sally: Ben, Christmas doesn't just come like that. It's more than all this.
 (Arm sweeps to indicate tree and gifts.)
Ben: I don't understand. More than
 The trees and lights and presents, and . . .
Jared *(kneeling beside Ben):* Much more Ben and more important.
Ben: Oh, tell me. Tell me please!
Sally *(shaking finger):* You're just trying to get out of going to bed.
Ben: I really want to know.
Sally: You must. You forgot to rhyme.
Jared: Tell you what, Ben. How about reading about the first Christmas?
Ben: Not as good as being here.
Sally *(grinning):* But almost as near.

(Ben and Jared groan.)

Jared: Sally, please hand me that Bible. Ben, you come and sit beside me
 on the sofa.

*(Sally hands Jared the Bible and sits on the other side of Ben. Jared reads Luke
2:1-7 and Isaiah 7:14. Fade out.)*

Scene 2

*Nativity setting. Scene opens on Mary and Joseph hovering over a manger.
Preschoolers file on stage, holding cards with a picture of Jesus on one side and,
when flipped over, spell out J-E-S-U-S. The phrase for each letter can be recited
by one or more children.*

J	J is for Jesus, who left His throne on high.
E	E is for Earth where He came to live and die.
S	S is for the Shepherds, who hurried to Bethlehem's stall,
U	U is for Us *(Pointing.)* you and you and me, For Jesus came for all.
S	S is for Salvation. Jesus came to save each one.
All:	For the baby of the manger *(Loudly.)* is Jesus Christ, God's Son!

Song: "Away in a Manger" (*Children form a semicircle around the manger and sing before returning to their parents.*)

Jared: Luke 2:8-16 (*Reads from Scripture as shepherds slowly find their way down the aisle to the manger.*)

Song: "How Great Our Joy!" (*First three stanzas by three or more singers as Primaries, first and second graders, file on stage, forming two groups, one on either side and half-facing nativity.*)

Group 1:	Shepherds heard the angels
	Sing of the Savior's birth.
Group 2:	The very Son of God,
	Came for love to earth.
Group 1:	As the angels left them,
Group 2:	The shepherds, though dirty and worn,
	Rushed to the dusty stable,
All:	To worship the child, newly born.
Group 2:	The shepherds somehow understood,
Group 1:	That the baby born that night,
All:	Was the Savior, the Messiah,
Solo:	Sent to bring us light.

Song: "Silent Night! Holy Night!" (*Primaries. Group 1—stanza 1, Group 2—stanza 2, All—stanza 3. When finished, file off stage.*)

Scene 3

Contemporary setting.

Ben: Christmas couldn't have begun
  Without Jesus Christ, God's only Son.
Sally: That's right, Jesus came you see,
  Because of you and me. Oh, no! Now I'm doing it.
Jared: What?
Sally: Rhyming wit. No! I've got to stop it. (*Scrunches up her nose.*)

Ben (*giggling*): Sally, you sound so funny, copying me.

Sally: G-r-r-r. (*Then grins.*) I'm not copying, but following . . . Jesus, that is.

Jared: That's what the shepherds did. After seeing Jesus, their lives took on a whole different meaning. Let's read what happened. (*He reads Luke 2:17, 18. Fade out.*)

Scene 4

Nativity setting. Juniors come on stage and form two lines facing each other across the stage. The first person from each line steps toward center stage. Each speaks a line in rap—short, snappy dialogue, with appropriate actions, then retires to the end of the line. To accommodate more juniors, two or more can speak each line.

Group 1a: You see, God had a marvelous plan

Group 2a: To save us from our sin.

Group 1b: He'd send His only Son to earth,

Group 2b: That we might come to Him.

Group 2c: He didn't come just as a baby,

Group 1c: But to offer us life brand-new,

Group 2d: He sacrificed His life for ours,

Group 1d: Jesus died for me and you.

Group 1e: From His sacrifice came life.

Group 2e: Jesus proved stronger than the grave,

Group 1f: Strong enough to conquer death,

Group 2f: Loving enough to save.

All: John 3:16

Group 2g: Yes, Jesus came that we may choose,

Group 1g: Whether or not to follow Him,

Group 2h: Ask Him to forgive us,

Group 1h: And ask Him to live within.

Group 1i: That's the "more" to Christmas,

Group 2i: God's plan for you and me,

Solo: The reason for the season,

All: Life with Him eternally.

(*All file off stage.*)

Scene 5

Contemporary setting.

Jared *(reads):* Luke 2:19, 20.

Ben *(jumping up from the sofa):* I see! I see! Christmas is much more than presents, lights, and a tree. Jesus came for ME!

Sally: That's right, Ben. And because He came, He understands all about our problems and hurts and sin.

Ben: All those bad things we do?

Sally: Like not going to bed when Mom says . . . ummm.

Jared: That's why Jesus died, to take our place and offer us forgiveness if we love Him and accept Him as our Savior.

Ben: Do you think that means me too?

Sally: Oh, yes, Ben. *(Hugs him.)* Jesus came for us all. He wants us to love Him and follow Him.

Jared: Jesus is waiting for you right now, Ben. He wants you to accept Him and follow Him.

Ben: Jesus, thank You for coming,
   As a babe on Christmas Day.
   Thank You for coming to take my sin
   By giving Your life away.
   Now at this Christmas season,
   I give my life to You,
   That I might have the greatest gift,
   Eternal life with You. Amen.

Song: "Thou Didst Leave Thy Throne" *(As Ben gets up, Sally, Jared, Mary, Joseph, Shepherds, Primaries and Juniors join him on stage to sing. Stanza 1: Ben, Sally, Jared; stanza 2: Mary, Joseph and Shepherds; stanza 3: Primaries; stanza 4: Juniors; last stanza: All. Then everyone files off stage leaving Sally and Ben.)*

Sally: Ben. It's time for bed.

Ben: Do I have to?

Sally: What would Jesus do?

Ben: Oh, all right. *(Grins at audience.)* Merry Christmas!
   (Leaves with Sally.)

CELEBRATE!

Judy Carlsen

This Christmas program, Christmas customs from around the world, is designed for a smaller church or group to perform. It is geared toward children from preschool through fifth or sixth grade. Props are simple; no special costumes are needed.

(Narrators can either stand off to one side of the stage when speaking or be unseen.)

Narrator 1: Children all over the world celebrate Jesus' birthday. Every country has its own special way of making Christmas special. Children everywhere love babies. Often they picture the baby Jesus as looking like themselves!

Narrator 2: And indeed He did! We are all made in God's image. Even though Jesus was born a Jew, He was and is more than just a Jewish baby; He is God. God has no nationality.

Narrator 1: We in the United States have borrowed customs from all over the world. Our borrowed Christmas symbols can help us remember the true meaning of Christ's coming to earth.

Narrator 2: Tonight we are going to be traveling to three areas of the world to see from which countries some of our cherished Christmas symbols come.

(Preschool and Kindergarten classes come up on stage as Narrator speaks. Four children carry a flat board with Mary and Joseph on it. Mary is riding a donkey. These figures can be either large-size standing cardboard cutouts or perhaps large plastic figures.)

Narrator 1: First, we go south of the border to Mexico where Christmas begins on December 16 and lasts for nine days. People in Mexico attend a posada *(poe-SAH-da)* each evening. Posada means "inn or resting place."

(Those children carrying Mary and Joseph are joined by half of the other children These are the Pilgrims. They stand to one side of the stage, while the rest of the

children stand on the other side. They are the Innkeepers. The Pilgrims walk over together to the Innkeepers. Pilgrims pretend to knock on the door.)

Innkeepers: Who knocks at my door?
Pilgrims: We are pilgrims, without shelter.
Innkeepers: No room! We are filled up.
Pilgrims: It's so cold, and we're tired!
Innkeepers: Who are you?
Pilgrims: Joseph of Nazareth, a carpenter, and his wife, Mary.
Innkeepers: You may stay in my stable tonight.

Song: "Away in a Manger" *(with motions)*

Narrator 1: Each night for eight nights, children go to a different friend's house and the posada is acted out. There is a happy party after the innkeepers allow the pilgrims to enter the house. Blindfolded children take turns trying to hit the hanging pinata *(pin-YAH-to)* with a stick.

(One child holds up a colorful pinata for all to see.)

Narrator 2: When the pinata finally breaks, candy and small toys come pouring out for all the children.
Narrator 1: On the ninth night, Christmas Eve, a little manger and some shepherds are added to the posada figures. After a time of prayer, the figure of the Christ child is placed in the manger.

Song: "Happy Birthday to You" *(using Jesus' name)*

(Children leave stage by using left steps. First, second and third graders come up on stage using right steps. Pianist plays "Happy Birthday to You" again.)

Narrator 2: Yes, happy birthday, Jesus! The creche or nativity scene is central to our celebration of Christmas. Although it originally came from Italy, Central and South American countries have adopted it wholeheartedly.
Narrator 1: Over 750 years ago, in 1224, St. Francis of Assisi was inspired to have a real enactment of the birth of Christ, with people playing the

parts of Mary and Joseph, the shepherds and angels. Live cows and donkeys also took part. This "living nativity scene" was a smash hit and became a tradition for the area. Today, some churches in the United States do the same thing.

Narrator 2: Now we travel to Germany where the Advent season begins on December 1. "Advent" means Christ's coming to earth.

(Two students hold up a large Advent calendar.)

Student 1: An Advent calendar marks the days in December until Christmas. Children in Germany begin each day by opening up the door marked with the day's date.

Student 2: Inside, they find a picture or Scripture verse about Christmas. Today, December _____ says: "Immanuel, which means God with us."

(Students 3 and 4 hold up Advent wreath or picture of one.)

Student 3: The Advent wreath is another special part of Christmas in Germany. On the first Sunday of December, one of the candles on the wreath is lighted. Each following Sunday another candle is lighted. On Christmas Day the final, middle candle marking Jesus' birth is lighted.

Student 4: The wreath is made of evergreen boughs. They stand for eternal life. Like a circle, God has no beginning and no end. The prophet Isaiah wrote: "Arise, shine; for thy light is come" (60:1). Christ came as that light.

Student 5 *(pointing to lighted Christmas tree in front of the church)*: Even our familiar Christmas tree is part of our country's heritage from Germany. One Christmas Eve the famous reformer, Martin Luther, walked home and was inspired by the beauty of thousands of stars twinkling in the clear night sky. When he arrived home, he cut down a fir tree and covered it with small candles for his children to see.

Student 6: Luther told his children the sparkling lights looked like the heavens on the night when Christ came to earth. The Christmas tree is a symbol of Christ, who is Life.

Student 7: Jesus said, "I am come that they might have life, and that they might have it more abundantly" (John 10:10).

Student 8: Another important German contribution to our Christmas celebration is music—Christmas carols!

Songs: "O Christmas Tree" and "Silent Night! Holy Night!"

(Children leave stage by left steps. Older children come up right steps onto stage. Pianist can continue quietly playing "Silent Night! Holy Night!")

Narrator 1: Our final stop this evening is in India. The Bible tells us that wise men from the east followed a special star to Bethlehem where they worshiped the child Jesus.

Narrator 2: We do not know exactly where these men came from or even how many there were. But we do know that they found Jesus when He was a young child, probably around two years old—not as a baby.

Student 1 *(holding up a paper star):* Indian Christians highlight the star in their Christmas celebration. They often place a paper one at the top of their Christmas tree—usually a banana tree—not the fir tree we have. When the wise men saw that special star they rejoiced with great joy, because it led them to Jesus.

Song: "We Three Kings of Orient Are"

Student 2: The wise men brought three special gifts to Jesus. One was gold. *(He holds up "gold," perhaps a brick spray-painted gold or even a gold necklace.)* This precious metal symbolizes Christ's kingship.

Student 3: The second gift was frankincense, a fragrant incense used in the temple. *(Holds up fancy bottle of "frankincense.")* This gift symbolizes Christ's role as priest. He was the link between God the Father and people.

Student 4: Myrrh was the third gift brought by the wise men. *(Holds up bottle of "myrrh.")* It is an unusual gift to give a young child—after all, it was used in burial to help preserve the body! This gift symbolizes Christ's sacrificial death for us.

Student 5: Gift-giving has, of course, become a major part of Christmas in the United States. But to whom are we giving gifts? How many people do you know who give gifts to Jesus on His birthday? What could we possibly give Jesus?

Student 6: Money is a great gift. We can give to organizations that help others in Jesus' name. Time is another gift to give Jesus. We can give an hour or two of free baby-sitting to someone who needs help, or go caroling to brighten up a shut-in's holiday.

Student 7: But the best gift we can give Jesus is ourselves. Remember that poem we learned as little children?
What can I give Him
Poor as I am?
If I were a shepherd,
I would give Him a lamb.
If I were a wise man,
I would do my part,—
Yet, what can I give Him,
Give my heart.

Student 8 *(holding up bells):* Bells are another major part of Christmas celebrations in India. Bells remind us that we should tell others about Christ's birth—the good news that He came to die for our sins. Indian people ring bells and sing as they walk to church on Christmas Day, gathering friends as they go.

Song: "Come On, Ring Those Bells"

(Children leave stage as narrators speak. Movie screen is put into place.)

Narrator 1: Well, it's been quite a whirlwind tour this evening—Mexico, Germany and India. We hope that when you see the many Christmas symbols we have mentioned this evening, you will remember why they are so important.

Narrator 2: We would like to close with a song that captures what we've been trying to say: Jesus loved us so much, He came to earth to die in our place and be our Light and Life.

(Slides or video of children from around the world are shown, while the song "Some Children See Him" is played. This is very effective with a soloist singing live or on tape.)

Best Pageant Ever
Lillian Robbins

Characters:
Casting Director *(older boy or girl or adult)*
Bart, wise man
Sidney, wise man
Marsha, angel
Carol, angel
Mrs. Cameron
Wanda, shepherd
Kevin, shepherd
Jack, Joseph
Alysia, angel
Dennis, shepherd
Erica, angel
Scott, wise man
Angela, Mary
Innkeeper
Other angels
Parents: Narrator, lighting and sound director, make-up artist
Choir *(may be angels without robes)*
Optional, more shepherds or wise men
Soloist

Settings:

Act I:	Outdoors
Act II:	Auditorium
Act III:	Bethlehem/Stable
Act IV:	Home in Bethlehem

Props: bushes or trees, clipboard, paper and pen, chaise, beanbags or mats, shepherds' crooks, spotlight, manger, hay, baby, stool, gifts, couch or lounge

Costumes: costumes for angels and nativity characters

Act I

Outdoors scene with bushes or tree decorations. Bart and Sidney enter, walking toward exit.

Sidney: Bart, I just don't know about this audition deal. I've never done anything like this before.

Bart: But I thought you liked to be in plays.

Sidney: I do. It's really cool acting like some character different from myself.

Bart: Well, then, what's your problem?

Sidney *(stopping):* I could be a cowboy or a radio announcer or a football coach, but a Christmas pageant is something else; to be a wise man or shepherd or some person like that. I just don't know.

Bart: Oh, come on, man. You'll be just great. You'll dress up like guys who lived in Jesus' time and that will get you in the mood.

Marsha *(calling out as she approaches):* Hey, guys. Where are you going? *(Catches up with them.)*

Bart: I'm still trying to convince Sidney to go with me to audition for the Christmas pageant.

Marsha: Oh, you mean the town pageant that's going to be the big affair at the community house?

Sidney: That's the one. And I just don't know if I can do it.

Marsha: Sure you can, Sidney. You know if Bart can do it, you can do it. I've seen you in plays before.

Bart: I keep telling him he'll be great.

Sidney: Oh, all right, I'll see how it goes. But if I don't like it, I won't do it.

Marsha: I'm on my way over there too. Come on, I'll walk along with you guys.

Carol *(calling):* Marsha, wait for me. *(Catching up.)* I want to talk to you.

Marsha: Okay. *(To boys.)* Just go on, fellows. I'll see you later. *(Boys leave.)*

Carol: I need some advice, Marsha. Mom thinks I ought to be in the Christmas pageant at the community building, but I'm afraid to go up for an audition.

Marsha: What's to be afraid of, Carol? Nobody's going to hurt you.

Carol: Sometimes I've seen Mary sing a song in a play like that. Suppose I have to sing a song. You know I can't carry a tune.

Marsha: Carol, don't you know that Mary is just one of the characters? There will be lots of others. Besides, you can sing. I've heard you.

Carol: But a solo? I'd be scared to death.

Marsha: Why don't you try out to be an angel? There will be a host of angels singing together. You won't mind doing that, would you? *(Taking her hand.)* Come on, Carol, and go with me. I'm on my way there now.

Carol: I guess I'll try it. Just to please my mom. *(Leaves.)*

Mrs. Cameron *(entering holding hands of two children):* Come on, kids. We don't want to be late.

Wanda: Mom, you promised me an ice cream cone.

Mrs. Cameron: That's after the audition. We must do important things first. If we don't get there on time, you may not get a part. Now we really must hurry.

Kevin *(speaking with a lisp):* Mom, thaut I do ip they asp me to speat?

Mrs. Cameron: You're just going to try for a shepherd's part, Kevin. You won't have to speak. You'll be an adorable little shepherd. Come on now. We'll all have ice cream later. *(Leaves.)*

Jack *(coming on stage with Alysia, Dennis, and Erica following):* Come on, kids. I knew you were going to make me late. Why do I have to take you kids with me anyway?

Dennis: You have to take us because Mom said so.

Alysia: And we're too little to go alone.

Erica: Mom was afraid for us to cross the street by ourselves, and she had to stay home with the baby.

Jack: I know. I know. But I could make a lot better time if I was going alone. In fact I'd already be there by now. Come on and walk a little faster. Maybe we'll get there before they have finished choosing all the parts. I really did want to have a chance of getting Joseph's part.

Alysia: I'm going to be an angel.

(They all leave the stage. Scott walks in reading a leaflet.)

Angela *(entering):* Scott, what are you reading?

Scott: It's just a copy of that leaflet about the audition for the Christmas pageant.

Angela: I guess you're going to be Joseph?

Scott: I don't know. I think I'd like that, but you know people from all the churches in town probably will be trying out. There may be other guys who want to be Joseph too.

Angela: But they really should choose you Scott. Nobody could be as good a Joseph as you.

Scott: I don't know. I guess we'll find out when we get there. How about you, Angela? Who do you want to be?

Angela: Oh, I'm trying out for Mary. I have always wanted to be Mary, ever since I was a tiny little girl.

Scott: I guess we better get along if we don't want to be late.

Angela: It really will be a wonderful Christmas celebration this year with everybody in town working together. *(Leaves.)*

Act II

Auditorium. All characters from Act I sit around stage, extra children dressed as angels sit together.

Casting Director: Okay, everyone. This is something different for all of us, and we want to have the best pageant ever. I'll tell you just how we're going to choose people to play each character. I think it's a good idea for an actor to really feel the part he is playing. To help me make good decisions, I want you to tell me something about the character you would like to play or why you would choose that part. Now, who wants to be a shepherd?

(Kevin and Dennis raise their hands.)

Director: All right, Dennis, why do you want to be a shepherd?

Dennis: Because I like to be outdoors like shepherds are when they watch their sheep. And I want to carry one of those crooks like shepherds use.

Director *(writes on clipboard as decisions are made):* Dennis, you'll do just fine. How about you, Kevin? Why do you want to be a shepherd?

Kevin: Jes cauph I can.

Director: You know what? I think you are absolutely right. You can be a shepherd too.

Wanda *(stands up):* Me too, Mr. Director. I want to be a shepherd.

Director: Wanda, don't you think boys are usually shepherds?

Wanda: But girls can be shepherds also. I know how to watch sheep. And besides, I want to be the first one to see baby Jesus.

Director *(concentrating):* Maybe if we dress you up and put your hair under a turban—ummm—Yes—I think it'll work. You can be a shepherd too. *(Speaking to group.)* Now, well, I think we have several girls who want to be angels. You are already dressed for it. Right, kids?

Angels *(except Carol, Alysia, Erica, with enthusiasm):* Oh, yes! We want to be singing angels.

Big Angel: I can be the biggest angel.

Little Angel: And I can be the littlest angel.

Director: That's settled then. All of you will be angels. Your costumes may need a little freshening up for the pageant.

Marsha: Me too. I want to be the first angel.

Director: What do you mean, Marsha, when you say first angel? And why do you choose that part?

Marsha: I have seen a play where the first angel came out to announce Jesus' birth, and she sang a beautiful song to the shepherds. I hope this angel will do that too. I love to sing.

Director: I'm sure you would make a beautiful angel, Marsha. Let me hear you sing a line or two of a song you like.

Marsha: How about *(Your choice. Marsha sings.)*

Director: That sounds great. Marsha will be the announcing angel. Now, how about Joseph?

(Bart and Jack stand.)

Director: Two Josephs? But, of course, we can have only one Joseph. Suppose each of you tell me why you want to be Joseph.

Jack: I know Joseph was a good man. He took care of Mary and found a place for them to spend the night. It was only a stable, but that was better than staying out on the road or in the yard. And I have experience looking after people because I look after my sisters and brother all the time.

Director: That's good reasoning. But I do have to choose between the two of you. Now, what about you, Bart? Why do you want to be Joseph?

Bart: I changed my mind. I'll just be a wise man with Sidney.

Director: Sidney, do you want to be a wise man?

Sidney: That will be cool. Do I get to wear a crown?

Director: I'm not sure yet just what you'll wear. Anyway, you and Bart will be wise men and Jack will be Joseph. Scott, what character do you want to play?

Scott: I'll be a wise man with Bart and Sidney.

Director: So now we have (*Looking at list.*) oh, yes, who wants to be Mary?

Angela: How about me? I can sing a good lullaby.

Director: Do you want to sing something for me now? How about a couple of lines of "Away in a Manger"?

Angela (*sings*): "Away in a Manger"

Director: Great! That takes care of that. Angela will be Mary. Now, what about you other girls? Who do you want to be?

Carol: I just want to be an angel like the girls over there. (*Points to group.*)

Alysia: We want to help sing with the multitude of the heavenly host.

Erica: I want to sing "Alleluia."

Director: Good, three more angels. (*Writing.*) Looks like we're pretty much finished here. But maybe you kids can help me find a few more helpers. We need somebody for a make-up artist.

Carol: My mom! She makes up all the time. (*Girls giggle. Carol calls out to audience.*) Come on up, Mom. (*Mom comes to stage.*)

Director: Thanks for helping. Now, we need a costume designer to be in charge of costumes.

Marsha: How about my mom? She sews real good. I'll ask her when I get home, and I know she'll say yes. We will have the best costumes a pageant ever had.

Director: I'll make a note of that, Marsha's mom—costumes. We are going to need a lighting and sound director.

Sidney: My dad's good with lights and mike setups. (*Calls to audience.*) How about it, Dad?

Dad: Sure! I'll do it.

Director (*calling out*): Thanks. We need a prop man too. There are several items we will need to set the scenes.

Bart: My dad can get anything you want. He will take care of that.

Director (*writes*): Bart's dad, prop man. (*Looks at list.*) Is that about all now? Oh, no. We must have an innkeeper.

Angela: My brother will be home from school. He has always been the innkeeper.

Director: Okay. Then I guess that's all except a narrator. We need a special man for that part. I hope we can get somebody who can talk nice and loud to be our narrator.

Dennis: My dad! He's loud all the time. (*Cast snickers.*)

Director: Then that's it, kids. See you Saturday morning at 10:00 A.M. (*All leave, Scott and Angela going out last.*)

Angela: Scott, I thought you were going to try out to be Joseph?

Scott: I was, but when I saw Jack stand up, I thought, "Hey, he really looks like a Joseph. He'll be a much better Joseph than I could be."

Angela: You're a great guy, Scott. You know that? (*Leaves.*)

Act III

Bethlehem/stable—lights low.

Joseph (*speaking to self as he approaches door*): I know Mary is tired. I do hope there will be a good place for her to rest.

(*Knocks on door three times. Lights little brighter.*)

Innkeeper (*coming out, speaking gruffly*): What do you want?

Joseph: I need room for my wife and myself.

Innkeeper: I don't have any room. We're full, wall to wall.

Joseph (*astonished*): But you can't be! There must be a place for Mary to lie down for a while.

Innkeeper (*emphatically*): I told you! I don't have any room!

Joseph: But my wife is expecting her first child any time now.

Innkeeper (*more considerate*): Oh? Where have you come from?

Joseph: All the way from Nazareth. That's where we live. I'm a descendant of David the king of Israel. So, of course, we had to come here to obey the decree put forth by Caesar Augustus for all of us to be taxed.

Innkeeper (*kindly*): Where is your wife now?

Joseph: With the donkey *(Points.)* back there by the big olive tree.

Innkeeper *(puts hand to head—thinking):* Umm!

Joseph: Maybe somebody would give up a place, just for Mary. I can get along all right out here under the stars.

Innkeeper: I just can't ask any of the people to do that. But I was just thinking. You could go down to the stable. There is fresh hay you can spread out for a bed. At least she would be sheltered for the night. *(Points.)* Just go out that way. You will see the stable just below the hill. *(Leaves, lights dimmed.)*

Joseph *(speaking as he leaves):* Is this God's way of providing for His Son's birth? Of course I must just trust His way.

Soloist: "O Holy Night!"

(Nativity scene is set up on stage. Mary and Joseph take their places, baby is laid in manger. Lights raised.)

Narrator: The animals at the stable must have been surprised when a man appeared and began clearing an area in their shelter. I wonder, was there perfect silence prevailing that night, or was mooing and braying heard across the airways? Animals have a keen sense of invasion of their privacy. Would they be disturbed very easily? What was that strange sound the animals heard, a baby crying? And their feeding trough, what was being laid there?

It was all happening there in the stable. And Mary brought forth her firstborn—a baby boy. But not just any baby boy. This was the only begotten Son of God. And His name was Jesus.

Mary: "Away in a Manger" *(Mary may hold baby in arms as she sings.)*

Narrator *(as Narrator speaks, shepherds position themselves on far side of stage):* Across the fields in the stillness of the night, sheep were secured in the fold and shepherds kept their night watch over them. Nothing unusual was expected to happen that night. *(Angel appears at side of stage—spotlight on angel.)* But suddenly a great light shone around them and an angel appeared to them.

Angel: Don't be afraid! I come to bring you good news of great joy, which shall be to all people. In the City of David, a special baby is born. This child is Christ the Lord, the Savior sent by God. You can find Him wrapped in swaddling clothes and lying in a manger.

(Host of angels appears, sings with announcing angel. Suggestion at end of play.)

All Angels *(in unison):* "Glory to God in the highest, and on earth peace, good will toward men" (Luke 2:14). *(Leaves. Spotlight off.)*

Narrator: The angels left the shepherds, who were bewildered by this amazing announcement. The baby—the anointed one of God, was born in Bethlehem just over the way. The shepherds talked about it. Surely they could go to Bethlehem. They could find the stable where the baby lay. This news had been sent to them by the Lord. It was the greatest thing that had ever happened in their lifetime. They would go right away.

(Shepherds come forward and bow before the manger, then take places nearby.)

Choir *(on side stage or behind the stage):* "Silent Night! Holy Night!"

Narrator: The shepherds were the first people to go to see Jesus, and when they had seen the wonderful miracle of God, they went forth telling what they had heard and seen. The people listened to the news and wondered at the message they heard. God's own Son was born in Bethlehem. And Mary kept all these things in her heart and thought about them again and again. *(Lights dim. Shepherds leave.)*

Choir: "What Child Is This?" *(Mary, carrying the baby, and Joseph leave; manger is removed.)*

Act IV

Home in Bethlehem.

Narrator: On the eighth day, when the child was circumcised according to the instructions given to Abraham, His name was called Jesus just as the angel had said, even before the baby was conceived.

Choir: "And They Called Him Jesus" *(or other name song)*

Narrator: No one knows exactly how old Jesus was when the men from the east followed the star of Bethlehem. *(Mary enters and sits on stool holding an older baby.)* The wise men came to Jerusalem asking, "Where is he that is born King of the Jews? for we have seen his star in the east, and are come to worship him" (Matthew 2:2).

Herod was troubled when he heard the words of the travelers, and he called the chief priests and scribes and other people, demanding of them where Christ should be born.

"They said unto him, In Bethlehem of Judea, for thus it is written by the prophet" (Matthew 2:5).

Choir: "O Little Town of Bethlehem"

Narrator: Herod asked the wise men when the star first appeared. "And he sent them to Bethlehem, and said, Go and search diligently for the young child; and when ye have found him, bring me word again, that I may come and worship him also" (Matthew 2:8).

The star went before the wise men until it came to the place where the young child was. There it stopped. The wise men came joyously into the house and reverently worshiped Jesus. They brought for Him gifts—treasures of gold, and frankincense, and myrrh.

Choir: "We Three Kings" *(Wise men enter, bow, present gifts.)*

Narrator: The wise men were "warned of God in a dream that they should not return to Herod, they departed into their own country another way" (Matthew 2:12). And the men from the east left Bethlehem. *(Wise men leave. Light shines on Joseph reclining on far side of stage.)*

Narrator: Joseph lay asleep when an angel of the Lord appeared to him in a dream. He was warned that Herod would try to find Jesus and destroy Him. The angel told Joseph to take Mary and Jesus to Egypt and stay there until he received word from God to leave that place.

In the darkness of night Joseph and Mary took Jesus and escaped to Egypt, where they lived until Herod was dead.

(Mary, carrying the child, and Joseph leave. Pause.)

Narrator: Jesus, the only begotten Son of God, was born among men to be the Savior of the world. *(Cast begins to assemble on stage.)* We gather here this evening to celebrate so great a Gift to all the world. I'll ask the audience to stand and join us in singing "O Come, All Ye Faithful."

Song: "O Come, All Ye Faithful"

Narrator: Let us pray.

(Short prayer, then cast sings "To God Be the Glory." Music continues as audience moves out.)

(Suggestion for angels' song.)

Host of Angels: "Joy to the world! the Lord is come; Let earth receive her King."

Announcing Angel: "Let every heart prepare Him room, and heaven and nature sing."

Host of Angels and Announcing Angel: "And heaven and nature sing, And heaven and heaven and nature sing."

Thanks for Jesus

Iris Gray Dowling

Purpose: This play will help children **learn** more about the first Christmas and be **thankful** that God sent Jesus.

Cast: Children in kindergarten to grade five. Fourteen children to recite a verse or poem. If there are not enough children, some children can do more than one part. Also needed are two small singing groups, bell band, and large singing group *(includes kindergarten through grade five).*

Props: Flannel board with Christmas border, bells or rhythm instruments, nine Christmas cards with the following pictures on them: *(These numbers correspond to the Child who holds card.)* #4. Angel appears to Mary; #5. Mary and Joseph traveling; #6. Mary and baby in stable; #7. Shepherds in the field; #8. Angel appears to shepherds; #9. Multitude of angels; #10. Shepherds at stable; #11. Shepherds tell everyone; #12. Wise men at nativity.

Introduction: Piano or instrumental solo to set the tone of thankfulness.

All Scripture passages are taken from the *King James Version.*

Suggested Songs: "Thank You, Lord," "Away in a Manger," "Silent Night! Holy Night!," "Go, Tell It on the Mountain," "Gospel Bells," "Joy to the World!" and others.

Teacher: We all need to give thanks to the Lord. Our children are going to present a Thanksgiving/Christmas program titled "Thanks for Jesus." First, we'll have a "Welcome" recitation by Child 1. *(Insert children's real names throughout.)*

Child 1 *(uses sign language for thanks, happy, tell, and listen; see notes on last page):*
Thanks for coming to our church,
For making this a joyous, happy day.
We'll do our best to tell good news,
So listen to what we have to say.

Teacher: The kindergarten class will do a Thankful Action Rhyme and sing "Away in a Manger." *(Class comes on stage.)*

Kindergarten *(uses hand motions for thanks, love, baby, and long):*
Thank You, Lord, for mommy and daddy.
Thank You for all my loving friends.
Thank You for sending baby Jesus
To Bethlehem's manger long ago.

Song: "Away in a Manger" *(by kindergarten class)*

Teacher: Our next recitation is a prayer by Child 2.

Child 2: "Thank You, Lord" *(Folds hands.)*
Let me take this time to say
To God in Heaven above:
Thank You for sending Your Son,
Thank You for mercy and love."
Thank You, Lord. Amen.

Teacher: Several children will sing: "O Give Thanks With a Grateful Heart" *(Suggested song.)*

Teacher: Thanksgiving is lots of fun. We have a big dinner with our families and talk about all we have to be thankful for. Boys and girls, do you know another song about giving thanks?

Children: Yes.

Teacher: Why don't we all sing it together?

Children: "Thank You, Lord"*(All classes go to the front and sing stanza 1 and refrain.)*

(After song, classes return to seats, except thirteen students who will participate in the Christmas Card skit. These sit on stage floor in a circle, except for Child 3. He/she remains standing.)

Teacher: Thanksgiving is a wonderful time to give thanks to God for all He's done for us in the past year. Child 3, did you want to say something?

Child 3: Yes. *(She recites.)*
Thanksgiving is here and gone
Christmas is coming soon;
Mom and Dad have a lot to get ready,
But I want to sing/play a Christmas tune.

(Child 3 sings or plays a Christmas solo.)

Teacher: I'm glad you're thankful God sent His Son, Jesus, and you want to tell us that story today. I see you boys and girls are getting your Christmas cards out. Some of you are reading them and writing notes to your friends. We can tell the Christmas story to others by the pictures and verses we read on the cards, can't we?

Children: Yes.

Teacher: Let's see if you can find the cards to tell the Christmas story found in Luke 1 and 2. Who can find the first card, which shows the angel appearing to Mary?

(Each child holds the card for audience to see. When he is finished speaking, place the card on the flannel board in correct sequence.)

Child 4 *(stands; holds card for all to see)*: Here it is.

Teacher: Child 4, will you say the verse on the card?

Child 4: "And the angel said unto her, Fear not, Mary: for thou hast found favour with God. . . . And Mary said, My soul doth magnify the Lord, And my spirit hath rejoiced in God my Saviour" (Luke 1:30, 46, 47). *(Shows card; puts card on the flannel board.)*

Teacher: Jesus wasn't born in Mary and Joseph's hometown of Nazareth. Who has a card and verse to explain why?

Child 5 *(stands, holding card)*: I do.

Teacher: Why don't you say the verse for us?

Child 5: "And it came to pass in those days, that there went out a decree from Caesar Augustus, that all the world should be taxed. . . . And Joseph also went up from Galilee, out of the city of Nazareth, into Judea, unto the city of David, which is called Bethlehem; because he was of the house and lineage of David: To be taxed with Mary his espoused wife, being great with child" (Luke 2:1, 4, 5). *(Child 5 places card on flannel board.)*

Teacher: Child 6, can you tell us what happened in Bethlehem?

Child 6 *(stands)*: "And so it was, that, while they were there, the days were accomplished that she should be delivered. And she brought forth her firstborn son, and wrapped him in swaddling clothes, and laid him in a manger; because there was no room for them in the inn"

(Luke 2:6, 7). *(Child 6 places card on board.)*

Teacher: Several children will sing "Silent Night! Holy Night!", stanza 1. Then the group on stage will sing stanza 2 with them.

Song: "Silent Night! Holy Night!"

Teacher: Who can tell us about the shepherds?

(Several children raise their hands.)

Teacher: Child 7, how about you?

Child 7 *(stands):* "And there were in the same country shepherds abiding in the field, keeping watch over their flock by night. And, lo, the angel of the Lord came upon them, and the glory of the Lord shone round about them: and they were sore afraid" (Luke 2: 8, 9). *(Puts card on board.)*

Teacher: What did the angels tell the shepherds, Child 8?

Child 8 *(stands):* "And the angel said unto them, Fear not: for, behold, I bring you good tidings of great joy, which shall be to all people. For unto you is born this day in the city of David a Saviour, which is Christ the Lord"(Luke 2: 10, 11). *(Places card on board in order.)*

Teacher: How many angels came to praise God? Do you know, Child 9?

Child 9 *(stands):* "And suddenly there was with the angel a multitude of the heavenly host praising God, and saying, Glory to God in the highest, and on earth, peace, good will toward men" (Luke 2: 13, 14). *(Puts card in order.)*

Teacher: What did the shepherds do about this important news? Child 10 and 11, will you tell us?

Child 10 *(10 and 11 stand together):* "As the angels were gone away from them into heaven, the shepherds said one to another, Let us now go even unto Bethlehem, and see this thing which is come to pass, which the Lord hath made known unto us. And they came with haste, and found Mary, and Joseph, and the babe lying in a manger" (Luke 2:15, 16). *(Places card on board.)*

Child 11: "And when they had seen it, they made known abroad the saying which was told them concerning this child. . . . And the shepherds returned, glorifying and praising God for all the things that they had heard and seen" (Luke 2:17, 20). *(Places card on board.)*

Teacher: The shepherds told the good news to everyone they met. We can tell the story of God's gift, Jesus, by the cards we send to our friends and neighbors and by the music we sing at Christmas. All the children will now sing "Go, Tell It on the Mountain."

Group Song: "Go, Tell It on the Mountain"

Teacher: Has anyone found a card telling about the wise men?

Child 12 and 13: We did. (*Both stand to recite.*)

Child 12: The wise men came to Bethlehem,
   They found the baby on that day,
   They brought some gifts of frankincense, gold, and myrrh.
   With joy they traveled on their way.

Child 13: If you haven't found the Savior yet,
   What better time than Christmas Day!
   Don't search the whole world over,
   When He's only one prayer away.

Teacher: Now we'll listen to our musical bells play while the classes sing "Gospel Bells."

(*Children ring bells each time they sing these words: "Gospel bells," "ring," and at the end.*)

Group Song (*with piano*): "Gospel Bells"

Teacher: Child 14 will give our closing invitation.

Child 14: We're glad you came to hear
   Our verses and songs of cheer;
   We hope we made our message clear,
   Please come back before next year.

Teacher: In closing, Child 15 will play a piano solo, "Joy to the World!"

Sign language motions as follows:
Thanks—Take fingers from mouth to others
Happy—Pat chest with right hand
Tell—Rotate index finger away from mouth
Listen (*hear*)—Point to ear
Love—Cross arms over chest

Happy Birthday, Jesus!

Judy Carlsen

This Christmas program celebrates Jesus' birthday in the mood of a birthday party. Streamers and balloons can decorate the stage or even the entire auditorium, if desired. The program is designed for preschool through fifth or sixth grade children to participate together. If your group is relatively small, each child can have a speaking part, if desired. It would be good if a decorated Christmas tree were on or near the stage, so that the "birthday gifts" can be placed under it until the time comes for that part in the program.

Introduction: All the children stand on stage together, with youngest ones in front of the group.

All: We're having a special party
To honor Christ our King.
You see it is His birthday,
And that is why we sing.

Song: "It's Jesus' Birthday" *(tune of "Jesus Loves Me")*
Christmas is a time of joy,
Great for every girl and boy.
But we must remember to
Give Him praise that is His due.

It's Jesus' birthday *(3 times)*;
We celebrate our King.

Speaker 1: We're having a birthday party for Jesus—and you are invited!
Don't worry—just come as you are!
Speaker 2: Parties always have games, so first we'll put together this
puzzle.

*Youngest children bring large pieces of puzzle of Jesus' face and put them in
place on upright board—on an easel, or with older children holding it. Use magnet on back of each piece onto metal board, or masking tape on cardboard pieces.)*

Speaker 3: Yes, it is a picture of our guest of honor, Jesus! It's His birthday!

Speaker 1: Now, we're going to play the game, "This Is Your Life."

(As speakers tell Jesus' life story, smaller children expose cards with symbols on them, so the audience can see.)

Speaker 1 *(picture of a circle):* There's really no beginning to Jesus' life. He always existed, because He is eternal God. Like a circle, Jesus has no beginning and no end.

Speaker 2 *(picture of manger or baby Jesus):* Jesus came to earth as a baby. That's what Christmas is all about. God with us—Immanuel.

Speaker 3 *(picture of Jesus as a young boy or with the teachers in the temple):* Jesus grew in every area of life—His physical body, His mind and His soul. When He was twelve, Jesus shocked the rabbis with His knowledge of God's Law.

Speaker 4 *(picture of hammer or carpenter):* Jesus learned to be a carpenter. That's how He made His living.

Speaker 5 *(picture of Jesus being baptized):* When He was thirty, Jesus was baptized by John in the Jordan River. He fasted for forty days in the desert and overcame Satan's temptation to sin. This was the start of His public ministry.

Speaker 6 *(picture of Jesus with the twelve disciples):* Jesus chose twelve men to be His disciples. He trained them to spread the good news and show God's love.

Speaker 7 *(picture of Jesus healing someone):* Jesus healed the sick and even raised the dead! He preached wherever He went. The Jewish leaders were quite upset with Him.

Speaker 8 *(picture of the crowd yelling, "Crucify Him!"):* The leaders had Jesus arrested because He said He was God. They swayed those in charge to have Jesus sentenced to be crucified.

Speaker 9 *(picture of Jesus dying on the cross):* Jesus hung on a cross. He died with two thieves. He took all the weight of all our sins. But that's not the end of the story!

Speaker 10 *(picture of the empty tomb and/or the resurrected Jesus):* On the third day, Jesus came alive again!

Speaker 11 *(picture of Jesus ascending to Heaven):* Forty days after He arose, Jesus returned to Heaven to take His rightful place with God the

Father. He lives forever, waiting for those who love Him to join Him.

Speaker 1: Yes, Jesus, this **is** Your life. You are alive forevermore.

Song: "Hallelujah, Jesus Is Alive" *(by Ron Kenoly, Integrity Music)* or "He Is Lord"

Speaker 2: Too often at Christmas, we all give gifts to each other. We receive gifts from friends and family. But Christmas is Jesus' birthday. Where are His gifts? What could Jesus possibly want or need from us?

(Each child picks up a brightly colored birthday package from under the Christmas tree. Each one opens it and displays an object or picture. If desired, the inside of each box top can have the child's part pasted in as a help.)

1: *(Pulls out picture of a head or even a wigstand "head")*
Loving God must come first.
God wants to have my mind.
When I let Him be tops in my life,
I'll be joyful, loving and kind.

2: *(Shows picture of eyes or a pair of glasses)*
To see what's good and true,
I know God wants my eyes.
The Bible is the best to read
To make me strong and wise.

3: *(Displays picture of ears or headphones)*
I'll listen for God's voice,
So I'll give the Lord my ears.
He speaks to me each time I pray.
He quiets all my fears.

4: *(Displays a microphone or a picture of a mouth)*
I'll sing and talk for Jesus.
My gift to Him is my voice.
My words should all be pleasing,
So my Father can rejoice.

5: *(Shows photograph of hands or real pair of gloves)*
To do good deeds for Jesus,
I need to give my hands.
I serve the ones around me
Or those in other lands.

6: *(Shows picture of feet or actual pair of shoes)*
I'll travel where God leads
With my last gift—my feet.
He guides wherever I should go.
His wisdom can't be beat!

7: *(Shows picture of whole body)*
From head down to my toes,
Jesus wants all of me.
My heart, soul, mind and strength,
To be all He wants me to be.

Song: "My Christmas Gift" *(tune of "Twinkle, Twinkle Little Star")*
I will give my Christmas gift
To the Lord for He is good.
God loved me so much He sent
Jesus down to take away my sins.
Now I want to give to Him
All myself this Christmas Day.

Speaker 1: Every birthday party has a cake, right? So here is Jesus'
birthday cake.

(A couple of older children bring out a Christmas tree cake with jelly beans as ornaments or a star-shaped cake. This can be a real or a fake cake.)

Song: "Happy Birthday to You!" *(using the name "Jesus")*

Speaker 2: There's only one candle to blow out, because Jesus is complete
and perfect. He's number one!

Speaker 1: We've celebrated Jesus' birth today. That's what Christmas is all about. Jesus came to earth to show God's love. He lived a perfect life.

Speaker 2: Jesus took the load of all our sins and died for us. Hallelujah, He came alive again, overcoming death's power. Thank You, Jesus, for coming to earth to save us from our sin!

Song: "Happy Birthday, Jesus!" *(by Carol Cymbala, Carol Joy Music 1995. Either children with soloist can sing this, or play a recorded version sung by the Brooklyn Tabernacle Choir.)*

Welcome to the Little King

David Woodward

A Christmas play for Junior Church

Characters:
Joseph
Mary
Shepherds
People to bring gifts
Guard
Simeon
Anna
Choir

Scene 1: Manger Scene
Scene 2: City gate of Jerusalem
Scene 3: Temple Courtyard
Scene 4: House in Bethlehem

Choir: "Tell Me the Story of Jesus" *(first stanza)*

Scene 1

Manger in Bethlehem. Mary is holding the Christ child in her arms, humming a Jewish lullaby. Joseph enters.

Joseph: Two of the shepherds that came the night our Son was born are coming to see us. That is, to see Him!

Mary: He's sleeping now, but they are welcome. *(Continues humming.)*

Joseph: I still have trouble realizing that our child is the Christ child, the King we have been waiting for! What a responsibility—to protect Him to care for Him, to teach Him and train Him! I'm just a carpenter.

Mary: Well, I'm just a young woman without much experience. I'm so glad I have someone older like Elizabeth to advise and encourage me.

But God has been our help in times past, and we can count on His wisdom to bring this child up so that He pleases Him in every way. Oh, the shepherds are outside! Do go greet them! *(She resumes her humming song to her baby Son.)*

(Shepherds arrive. They enter quietly and stand watching the child.)

First Shepherd *(to his partner):* The mother's heart is singing. It reminds me of the angels.

Second Shepherd: I've heard you singing more the last few days than you ever have before. We all are glad!

First Shepherd: No wonder! We have been blessed to see heavenly glory and all because of this special child. *(He turns to Joseph.)* And Joseph, what name will you give the child on the eighth day after His birth? Have you chosen it? It must be special. The angels told us that He is the promised Messiah, Christ, the Lord.

Joseph: He is very special, my friends, so I have not chosen His name. God chose the name, and an angel of God came to tell me that I am to give Him the name JESUS. The angel said this name with its meaning of SAVIOR is the right one for Him because He will save His people from their sins.

First Shepherd: Save us from our sins? Why, most people think He will save us from the Romans! Or from King Herod's tax collectors!

Second Shepherd: Hush! Someone might hear you and report you to Herod. He has no love for other kings.

Mary: An angel came to me to tell me that God was giving me this very special Son, telling me that He would be great and will be called the Son of the Most High. And the angel told me not to be afraid.

Joseph: Yes, we have nothing to fear as long as we stay close to the Lord God. He has a wonderful plan for us all.

First Shepherd: Thank you, Joseph. We believe that. Well, we need to get back to our sheep. We will come back to celebrate with you when you name the child.

Joseph: Peace be with you!

Scene 2

City gate of Jerusalem, three weeks after the naming of Jesus. Two or three people pass a Roman guard who looks into their baskets. Joseph, carrying Jesus, and Mary approach the gate.

Guard: Who are you, and what is your business?

Joseph: I am Joseph from Bethlehem. I go to the temple with my firstborn Son.

Guard *(turning to Mary):* And what are you holding? *(She lifts up a basket.)* Huh! Two pigeons. Go on! Go on! *(They move through the gate.)*

Joseph *(to Mary):* This is the first time our Son has come into Jerusalem, but it will not be the last time!

Mary: Would that He were more welcome than He was today! The angel told me that the Lord God will give Him the throne of David and that His kingdom—that of our little Jesus—will never end. How far He seems from that today, and yet God has given us many signs. I hope that the Lord will give us another sign today as we go up to His temple.

Scene 3

Within the temple courts. Joseph, carrying Jesus, and Mary come in from one side. Simeon approaches them from the other side. Suddenly he smiles and raises his hands, then clasps them.

Simeon: I see that you come to follow the custom which the Law requires. Let me assist you in this that each of you may receive a blessing from God on high. As for me, this is a blessing for which I have long awaited. Please give me your Son.

Joseph *(as he hands over the Christ child)*: Praise God and give Him glory!

Simeon: What is His name?

Joseph: His name is Jesus, for He will save His people from their sins.

Simeon *(raising the baby up)*: Sovereign Lord, as You have promised, you now dismiss Your servant in peace, for my eyes have seen your salvation, which You have prepared in the sight of all people, a Light for revelation to the Gentiles and for glory of Your people Israel.

Joseph: Bless us, too, as we are parents and teach our Son.

Simeon: The Lord bless you and cause His face to shine upon you and give you peace. *(Turning to Mary.)* This child is destined to cause the falling and rising of many in Israel, and to be a sign that will be spoken against, so that the thoughts of many hearts will be revealed. And a sword will pierce your own soul, too. *(He turns and walks away a few steps and stands in prayer.)*

Joseph *(to Mary)*: What does this mean?

Mary: I don't fully understand, but God does all things well. Remember what he said about our Jesus—a Light to Gentiles, glory to our people Israel. What more could we desire?

Anna *(walking slowly up)*: Thanks be to God! He has showed me that this child is the One my friends and I have been looking for. He is the One who will redeem Jerusalem and set us free. Oh, I must go and tell them this good news! *(She leaves.)*

Joseph *(holding Jesus)*: O God, thank You for not only one sign but two. Now I ask of You that our Son may grow and become strong, filled with wisdom and Your Spirit. *(To Mary.)* Let us return to Bethlehem. *(They walk off.)*

Scene 4

Back in Bethlehem. Some time has passed and it is evening, and the stars are beginning to shine.

Joseph: Look, Mary, do you see that bright star? I have never noticed it before.

Mary: Nor have I. It's a new one. It is brighter than any of the other stars in the sky. God must have a hand in this.

Joseph: Stargazers say that a star like that means that a new and special king has been born.

Mary: If so, then it is another sign, for God made the stars and moves them as He wishes.

Joseph: And God brought us Jesus, our little King.

Mary: Not just ours. Jesus has come to be a blessing to all peoples.

Joseph: And the Scriptures say that they will come and will bring their gifts to Him. Think of it! What will it be like in years to come?

From all over the audience prepared individuals, perhaps eight to ten of them, rise and bring gifts forward and place them close to Jesus (Now in a crib rather than a manger or sitting on Mary's lap.)—food, flowers, clothes but also a musical instrument, a small computer, a tricycle, a book bag, etc. Or the gifts can represent various peoples and regions of the world. Last of all, one child brings up a large heart with "I LOVE YOU, JESUS" written on it. Afterwards, the Choir sings.

Choir: "Joy to the World!" *(first stanza)*

Audience joins in singing other stanzas of "Joy to the World!" Then sing, "For God So Loved the World"